Architecture 4

FOR KIDS

Today We Present Series

DR. HORACIO SANCHEZ

Architecture
For Kids 4

Today We Present Series

To Constanza, Andres, and Almudena
To Vera
To Cecilia, Patricio, Fernanda
To Friends and Family
To all Future Architects
To Art and Architecture
To those who believe

Leaving a Legacy

Dr. Horacio Sanchez
https://www.architectureforkids.net

contact@architectureforkids.net

Architecture for Kids 4 - Today We Present Series is a book about architectural elements, construction hand tools, heavy equipment, and construction professionals. Are you interested to learn about doors, windows, or chimneys? or what is a Hammer and when was it first used? Are you interested to know what an electrician does? You are going to find out about that and more in this amazing book!

A fun and visual way that I am sure you are going to enjoy.

This book is for you, future architect, or designer. If you decide to follow the architecture path, I can guarantee you that it will be a fantastic journey!

Dr. Horacio Sanchez

Today We Present Series

Contents

1. Architecture Elements

2. Construction Hand Tools

3. Heavy Equipment Series

4. Construction Professionals

5. INDEX

Architecture Elements

"The good building is not one that hurts the landscape, but one which makes the landscape more beautiful than it was before the building was built"

Frank Lloyd Wright

Architecture Elements

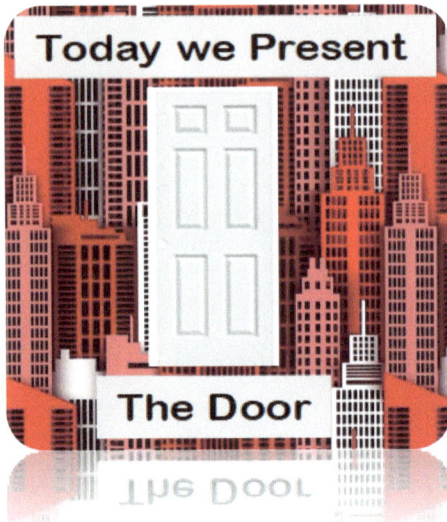

Today we Present

The Door

What is a Door?

A door is used as a barrier that allows the access in/out from a building / house and to provide security.

When was the first door used?

The First Door was found in Egyptian Paintings and Tombs.

Shapes / Materials?

Doors are fabricated in different shapes, colors, and materials.

Sizes?

The Largest Doors stand at 456 feet high and are 150 feet taller than the Statue of the Liberty and are located at NASA

Architecture
For Kids 4

Architecture Elements

Today we Present

The Window

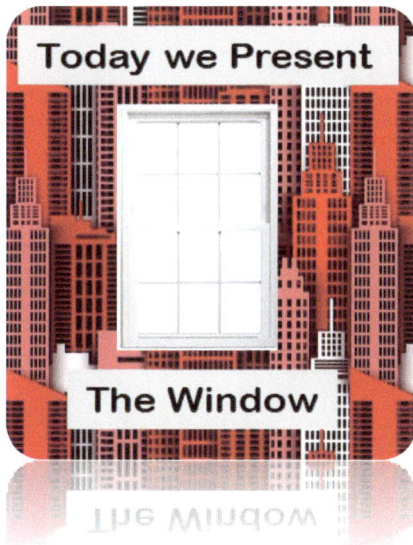

What is a Window?

A window is an opening in a wall, door, or roof that allows light and air to enter a building or home. Windows also provide security.

When was the first window used?

The Romans were the first to use glass

Shapes / Materials?

Windows are fabricated in different shapes, colors, and materials. Paper windows were economical and used in ancient China, Korea, and Japan. Rice paper was used to produce them.

Sizes?

The Largest Windows are normally found in airports, shopping centers, buildings.

Architecture For Kids 4

Today We Present Series

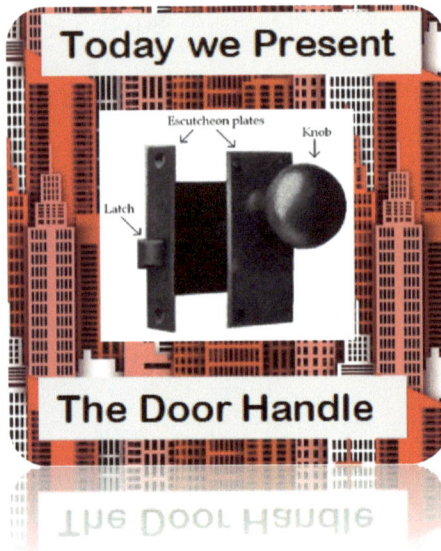

Today we Present

The Door Handle

Escutcheon plates
Knob
Latch

What is a Door Handle?

A door handle is an item installed on a door and it is used to open or close a door, pull, or push.

When was the first Door Handle used?

Door handles have been in existence since the Neolithic period. Key doorknobs exist since the Egyptian civilization.

Shapes / Materials?

Door handles are fabricated in different shapes, colors, and materials.

Design and Architecture

Architects and designers started to take serious interest in door handles, Peter Behrens, Walter Gropius, and Antoni Gaudi designed door handles.

Architecture Elements

Today we Present

The Cement

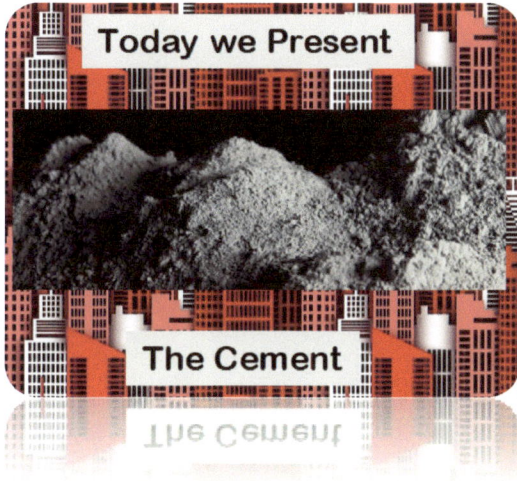

What is Cement?

Cement is a substance used in construction that hardens when mixed with water.

When was the first-time cement was used?

The first samples of cement are from twelve million years ago.

Cement can be traced back to the Roman Empire and it was made from crushed rock and burnt limestone.

Learning Fact

In Egypt stone blocks were pasted together with a glue made of sand and other burnt materials like gypsum.

Architecture Elements

Today We Present Series

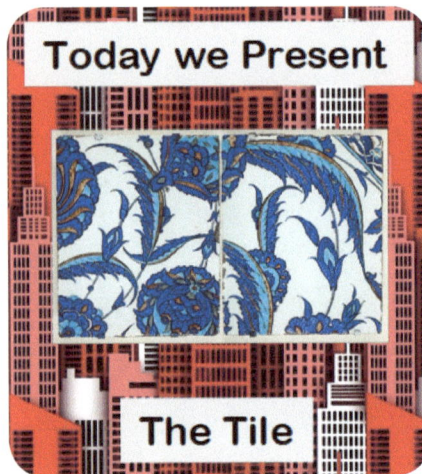

Today we Present

The Tile

What is Tile?

Tiles are thin objects usually square or rectangular in shape, painted or decorated. Tiles are often used in walls and floors.

When was the first Tile used?

The first tiles were discovered in the Elamite Temple (Khuzestan province of Iran) in the 13th century.

Shapes / Materials?

Tiles are usually made of ceramic, stone, metal, clay, or glass.

Learning Fact

Rooms with tiled floors made of clay decorated with geometric forms and patterns were discovered in houses and temples in India.

Architecture Elements

Today we Present

The Baluster

Today we Present Series

What is Baluster?

A baluster is a square, round, or twisted element used in stairways, barriers, balconies, and other architectural features.

When was the first Baluster used?

The earliest examples of balusters were found in Assyrian palaces. In Architecture was used in the early Renaissance period.

Materials?

Common materials used are wood, stone, metal, and in some cases ceramic.

Learning Fact

Baluster is derived through the French: "baluster", Italian: "balustro", Latin: "balaustium'.

Architecture Elements

Today we Present

The Column

The Column

Today we Present Series

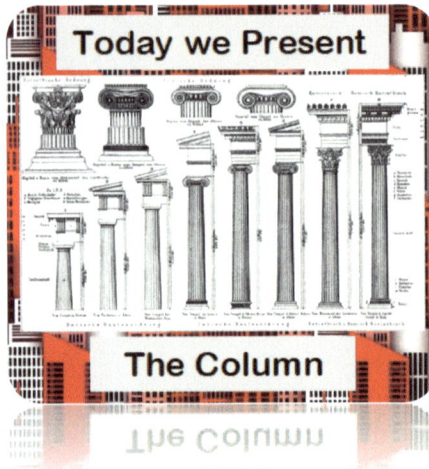

What is a Column?

A column is a structural element that transmits the weight of the structure above to other elements below.

When was the first Column used?

All significant Iron Age civilizations of the Near East and Mediterranean made columns. Some of the most elaborate columns in the ancient world were found in Persia.

Materials?

Common materials used are wood, and stone.

Learning Fact

The Egyptians, Persians and other civilizations mostly used columns for the practical purpose of holding the roof inside a building. The Ancient Greeks, followed by the Romans, loved to use Columns on the outside as well.

Today We Present Series

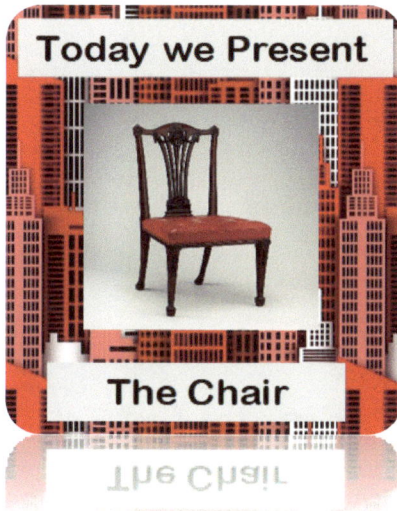

Today we Present

The Chair

What is a Chair?

A chair is one of the basic pieces of furniture. A chair is a type of seat made of two pieces, attached, and four legs in each corner.

When was the first Chair used?

Chairs are known from Ancient Egypt, the Greeks, and the Romans. They were in common use in China in the 12th century and used by the Aztecs.

Materials?

Common materials used are wood, stone, plastic, cement.

Learning Fact

Egyptian chairs appear to have been of great richness and splendor. Egyptians believed that the chairs need to represent natural forms to avoid creating chaos in the universe.

Architecture Elements

Today we Present

The Table

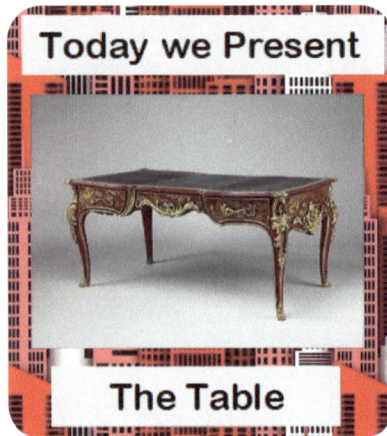

What is a Table?

A table is a piece of furniture with a flat top and one or more legs, used as a surface for work, eat or place things. Tables vary in shapes and sizes.

When was the first Table used?

Early tables were made and used by the Ancient Egyptians around 2,500 B.C., using wood.

Materials?

Common materials used are wood, stone, plastic, cement. Shape and size vary dependent on their use style or origin.

Learning Fact

The Greeks and Romans made more frequent use of tables, notably for eating, although Greek tables were pushed under a bed after use.

Architecture Elements

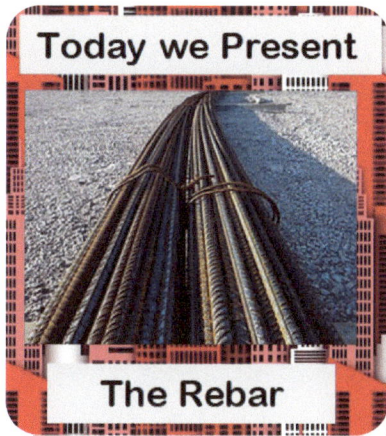

Today we Present

The Rebar

What is Rebar?

Rebar is a steel bar or mesh of steel wires used in concrete to strengthen and aid the concrete to support heavy weights.

When was the first Rebar used?

Rebar in construction have been used since at least the 15th century.

Materials?

The most common material in Rebar is carbon steel.

Learning Fact

Ernest L. Ransome, an English engineer and architect who worked in the United States, made a significant contribution to the development of reinforced steel in concrete. He invented the twisted iron rebar.

Today we Present

The Elevator

Today we Present Series

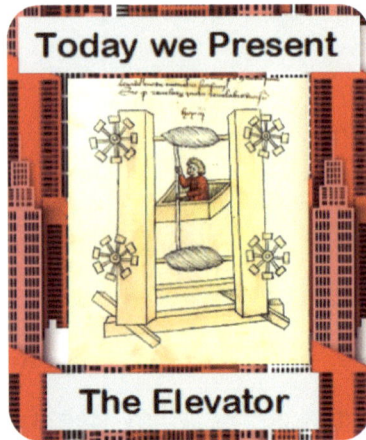

What is an Elevator?

An elevator is a vertical transport machine that moves people or cargo between floors, levels or other areas of a building, vessel, or other structure.

When was the first Elevator used?

The earliest known reference of an elevator is in the works of the Roman architect Vitruvius, who reported that Archimedes built his first elevator probably in 236 BC.

Materials?

The most common material in Elevators is steel, aluminum, and wood in some cases.

Learning Fact

In 1845, the Neapolitan architect Gaetano Genovese installed in the Royal Palace of Caserta (Italy) the "Flying Chair", an elevator ahead of his time.

Architecture Elements

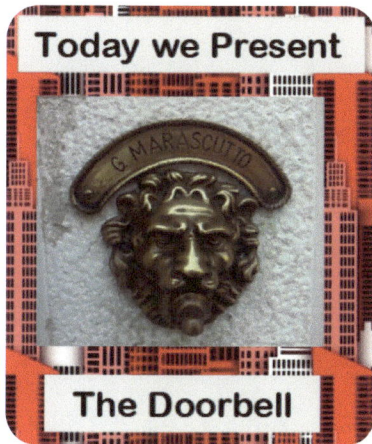

Today we Present

The Doorbell

Today We Present Series

What is a Doorbell?

A doorbell is a device typically installed near a door to a building entrance to notify someone's arrival.

When was the first Doorbell used?

Ancient Egypt, Romans, and Greeks.

Materials?

Although the first doorbells were mechanical, activated by cords, modern doorbells are electric and made of plastic or metal.

Learning Fact

Before electrical doorbells, large houses and estates often had complicated mechanical systems to allow occupants of any room to pull a bell cord and ring a bell at a central bell panel.

Architecture Elements

Today we Present

The Door Knocker

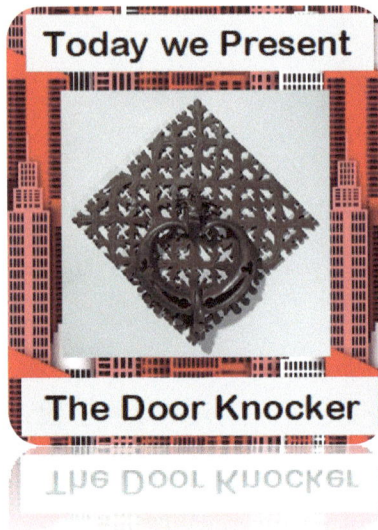

What is a Door Knocker?

A door knocker is an item of décor placed on doors that allows people outside a house or other building to alert those inside of their presence.

When was the first Door Knocker used?

The earliest known reference of door knockers was found in Ancient Egypt, Greek, Rome, and India.

Materials?

The most common material in door knockers is steel, metal, aluminum, or wood.

Learning Fact

German professor Franz Sales Meyer distinguished three kinds of door knockers: "the ring", the "hammer", and an ornate category with different shapes or figures.

Today we Present

The Brick

Today We Present Series

What is a Brick?

A brick is a type of block used in walls, pavements and other elements in architecture and construction.

When was the first Brick used?

The oldest discovered bricks were made from shaped mud and date back to 7,500 BC in the upper Tigris region in Mesopotamia.

Materials?

Bricks are produced in numerous classes, types, materials, and sizes.

Learning Fact

The Great Wall of China was made from 3.8 billion bricks.

Architecture Elements

Today we Present

Roof Tiles

Today we Present Series

What is a Roof Tile?

A roof tile is a type of curved shape block used in roofs to keep out rain and as an architectural element.

When was the first Roof Tiles used?

Tiled roofs first replaced wood roofs in Mesopotamia. The earliest findings of roof tiles in ancient Greece are documented from the temples of Apollo and Poseidon between 700 and 650 BC.

Materials?

Clay, Mud, concrete, plastic, terracotta, slate.

Learning Fact

In China, roof tiles are in use throughout the country on temples and village houses.

Architecture Elements

Today we Present

The Downspout

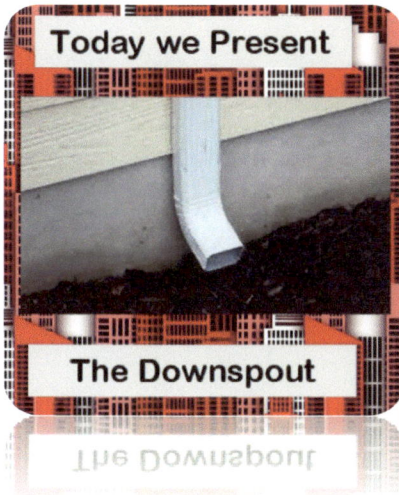

What is a Downspout?

A downspout or roof drainpipe is a pipe that carries rainwater from a rain gutter to ground level.

When was the first Downspout used?

The first downspout installed was in the year 1240 on the Tower of London, to protect the newly painted walls from the rain.

Materials?

Plastic, Metal, Aluminum, Copper, or Steel in some cases.

Learning Fact

The water is directed away from the building's walls or foundation to protect them from water damage.

Architecture Elements

Today we Present

The Rain Gutter

Today we Present Series

What is a Rain Gutter?

A rain gutter is a water collection channel installed in the roof of a building or structure and attached to a downspout.

When was the first Rain Gutter used?

The Romans brought rainwater systems to Britain. The technology was then used and re-designed by the Normans.

Materials?

Cast Iron, Lead, Zinc, Plastic, Steel, Copper, Aluminum, PVC, Concrete, Stone, or even Wood.

Learning Fact

The water is directed away from the building's walls or foundation to protect them from water damage.

Architecture Elements

Today we Present Series

Today we Present

The Nail (fastener)

What is a Nail?

In woodworking or construction, a nail is a small object made of metal, which is used as a fastener or to hang something.

When was the first Nail used?

The first nails were made of wrought iron. Nails date back to ancient Egypt, bronze nails found in Egypt have been dated 3400 BC.

Materials?

Iron, Plastic, Steel, or even Wood.

Learning Fact

The Romans made extensive use of nails. The Roman army, for example, left behind seven tons of nails when evacuated the fortress of Inchtuthil in Perthshire in the United Kingdom in 86 to 87 CE.

Architecture Elements

Today we Present Series

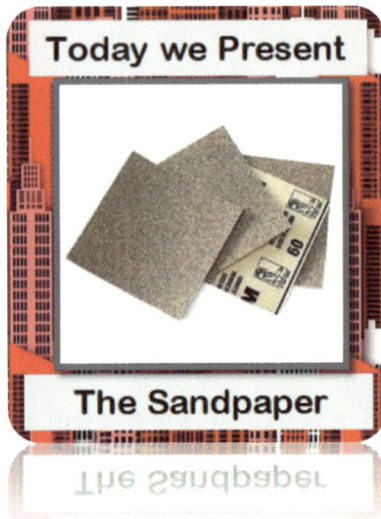

Today we Present

The Sandpaper

What is Sandpaper?

Sandpaper is a piece of paper or cloth with abrasive material glued to one face. It is used to remove material from surfaces for example in painting or wood.

When was the first Sandpaper used?

The first recorded instance of sandpaper was in 13th century China when crushed shells, seeds, and sand were attached together using natural gum.

Materials?

Sandpaper is produced in different sizes and types of grit (abrasive) material.

Learning Fact

Glass paper was manufactured in London in 1833 by John Oakey. In 1921, 3M invented a sandpaper with silicon grit and a waterproof adhesive, this allowed to use it with water.

Architecture Elements

Today we Present

The Chimney

Today We Present Series

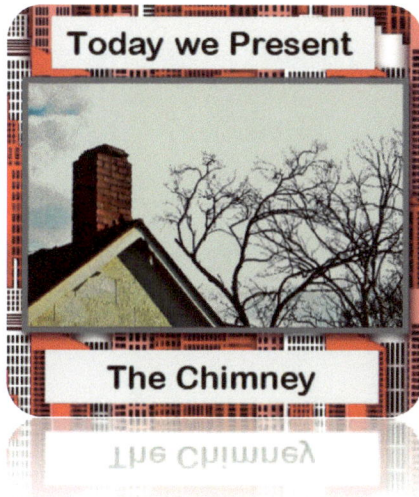

What is a Chimney?

A Chimney is a vertical architectural ventilation element usually installed in the roof of a structure used to release gases to the exterior.

When was the first Chimney used?

Chimneys use dates to the Romans that used tubes in the walls to let smoke out from their bakeries.

Materials?

Wood, Plaster, Mud, Brick, Stone, Metal, Concrete.

Learning Fact

Domestic chimneys first appeared in northern Europe in the 12th century. Industrial chimneys became common in the late 18th century.

Architecture Elements

Today We Present

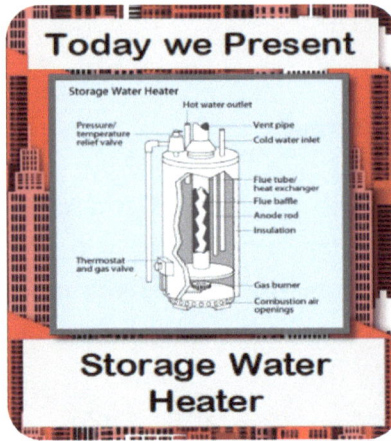

Storage Water Heater

Hot water outlet

Pressure/
temperature
relief valve

Vent pipe

Cold water inlet

Flue tube/
heat exchanger
Flue baffle
Anode rod
Insulation

Thermostat
and gas valve

Gas burner

Combustion air
openings

Storage Water Heater

What is a Water Heater?

A storage water heater is a domestic appliance that serves to heat and provide instantaneous hot water.

When was the first Water Heater used?

The first water heater was made by a man in England in 1868. He heated cold water by flowing it through pipes that were exposed to a burner of hot - - -

Materials?

Water heaters are made of steel and use natural gas, propane, or electricity.

Learning Fact

Storage water heaters are the most common type of water heating system in homes. A storage water heater can hold and provide 20 to 80 gallons of hot water.

Architecture Elements

Today We Present Series

Today we Present

The Drywall

What is a Drywall?

A drywall is a panel made of "gypsum" with additives between sheets of paper or fiber glass, used in construction of interior walls and ceilings.

When was the first Drywall used?

The first drywall plant in the UK was opened in 1888 in Rochester, Kent.

Materials?

Gypsum (soft sulfate mineral composed of calcium sulfate dihydrate), additives, paper, fiber glass.

Learning Fact

Drywall material, unlike wood, is not generally reusable once it has been removed from a home. Drywall typically ends up in landfills, which creates some environmental concerns.

Architecture Elements

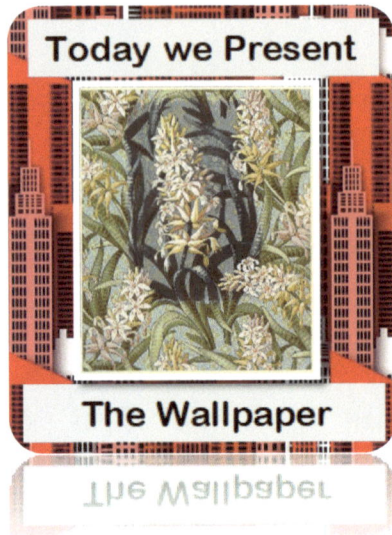

Today we Present

The Wallpaper

What is Wallpaper?

Wallpaper is a material used in interior decoration to decorate interior walls. It is usually sold in rolls and is applied onto a wall using wallpaper paste.

When was the first Wallpaper used?

England and France were leaders in European wallpaper manufacturing. Among the earliest known samples is one found on a wall from England and was printed in 1509.

Materials?

Paper, Plastic , Wood.

Learning Fact

The main historical techniques are hand-painting, woodblock printing, stenciling, and various types of machine printing. The first three date back to before 1700.

Architecture Elements

Today we Present

Faux Painting

What is Faux Painting?

In architecture or construction Faux Painting is a term used to describe decorative paint finishes that replicate the appearance of materials such as marble, wood, or stone.

When was the first Faux Painting used?

Faux painting experienced major resurgence in the nineteenth century and the Art Deco styles of the 1920's.

Materials?

Oil or Water based paint, and sealers.

Learning Fact

The term comes from the French word "faux" meaning false. Faux finishing in the decorative arts began with plaster and stucco finishes in Mesopotamia over 5,000 years ago.

Architecture Elements

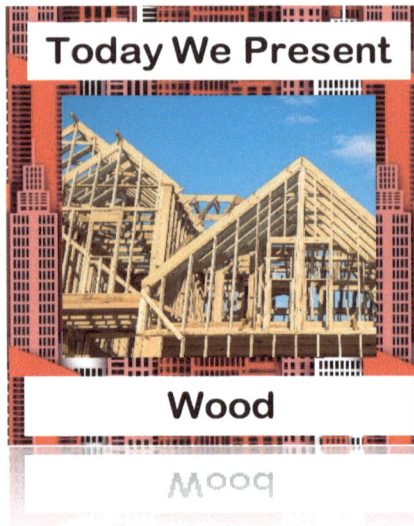

Today We Present

Wood

Wood

Today We Present Series

What is Wood?

Wood is the most famous material, and it is used around the world. It is a construction favorite because of its strength and flexibility.

When was Wood first used?

Evidence shows that wood was used to build houses 10,000 years ago.

Shapes?

Wood is cut and fabricated in different sizes, and types (Pine,

Interesting Fact

The Neolithic long house built around 6000 BC is one of the largest wood frame buildings of that era with the capacity to house around 30 people.

Architecture Elements

Today We Present Series

Today We Present

Paint

What is Paint?

Paint is a liquid used to protect, cover, provide color or texture to walls, ceilings, floors, stairs, furniture, etc.

When was Paint first used?

Paint is one of the earliest arts of humanity. Cave paintings drawn with vegetables, minerals colors and charcoal were made by early Homo sapiens 40,000 years ago.

Types?

Paint can be oil-based or water-based and each has distinct characteristics.

Interesting Fact

Acrylic Paints Take Between 10 Minutes to 2 Hours to Dry!

Construction Hand Tools

"The earliest known tools, found in 2011 and 2012 in a dry riverbed near Kenya's Lake Turkana, have been dated to 3.3 million years ago. The present array of tools has as common ancestors the sharpened stones that were the keys to early human survival. "

Joseph A. McGeough

Construction Hand Tools

Construction Tools Series

The Trowel

The Trowel

Today We Present Series

What is a Trowel?

A Trowel is a small hand tool used for digging, applying, smoothing, or moving material like cement.

When was the first Trowel used or invented?

Numerous forms of Trowels were used since the invention of the hand tools in the prehistoric.

Sizes? Materials?

Trowels vary in size and shape and the handle is normally found in wood.

Learning Fact

Selecting the right trowel depends on the type of work being performed.

Construction Hand Tools

Construction Tools Series

The Shovel

What is a Shovel?

A Shovel is a tool used for digging, lifting, and moving materials like sand, gravel, soil or to move snow.

When was the first Shovel used or invented?

In the Neolithic age and earlier, an animal bones were often used as shovels.

Sizes? Materials?

Shovels vary in size and shape and the handle is normally found in wood.

Learning Fact

In 1967, a wooden shovel from approximately 2000 BC was discovered in Turkey.

Construction Hand Tools

Construction Tools Series

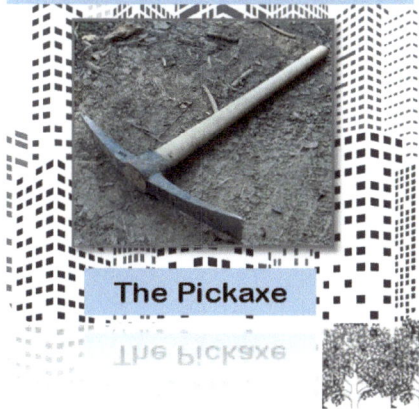

The Pickaxe

The Pickaxe

Today We Present Series

What is a Pickaxe?

A Pickaxe is a T-shaped tool that it is used for breaking, the head is normally metal.

When was the first Pickaxe used or invented?

In Prehistoric times a large bone of deer or a deer antler was used as a pointed pick.

Sizes? Materials?

A normal pickaxe handle is made of wood and is about three feet long and about 2.5 pounds.

Learning Fact

The Pickaxe was also used as a battle weapon in ancient times.

Architecture
For Kids 4

Today We Present Series

39

Construction Hand Tools

Construction Tools Series

The Wheelbarrow

Today We Present Series

What is a Wheelbarrow?

A Wheelbarrow is a hand vehicle with one tire used to transport or carry materials.

When was the first Wheelbarrow used or invented?

The Wheelbarrow may have existed in Greece. The first wheelbarrows in medieval Europe appear in 1170.

Sizes? Materials?

Handles are normally made of wood; the body is normally metal, but plastic is also used.

Learning Fact

The Wheelbarrow can be used in any activity, and it is found in farms or in cities.

Construction Hand Tools

Construction Tools Series

The Hard Hat

What is a Hard Hat?

A Hard Hat is like a helmet used in construction or other industries to protect the head from failing objects.

When was the first Hard Hat used or invented?

The Hard Hat may have existed in Greece, made of coconuts, leather and or wood.

Sizes? Materials?

Hard Hats are made of durable materials like metal, fiberglass, or hard plastic.

Learning Fact

Hard Hats are a personal protective equipment and require having penetration protection.

Construction Hand Tools

Construction Tools Series

The Hammer

What is a Hammer?

The Hammer is a tool consisting of a heavy head fixed to a long handle that is swung to deliver an impact to an object or area.

When was the first Hammer used or invented?

The use of simple hammers dates to around 3.3 million years ago. The first hammers were made of rocks attached to sticks or animal bones.

Sizes? Materials?

The handle is typically made of wood or plastic. The head is typically made of steel or hard rubber.

Learning Fact

Hammers are used for shaping, breaking and other applications.

Construction Hand Tools

Construction Tools Series

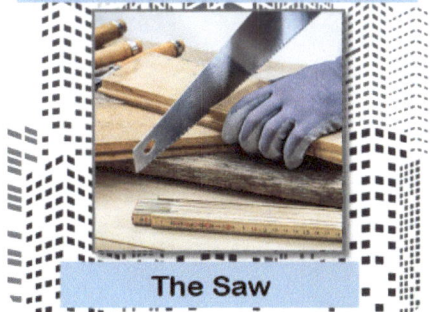

The Saw

What is a Saw?

A Saw is a tool with a blade, wire, or chain with tooths. It used to cut materials like wood, plastic, metal and sometimes stone.

When was the first Saw used or invented?

According to a Chinese legend the saw was invented by LuBan. In Greek mythology Talos the nephew of Daedalus invented the saw.

Sizes? Materials?

The handle is typically made of wood or plastic. The body is typically made of steel.

Learning Fact

In ancient Egypt, saws were made of cooper, as early as the Dynastic Period 100-2686 B.C.

Construction Hand Tools

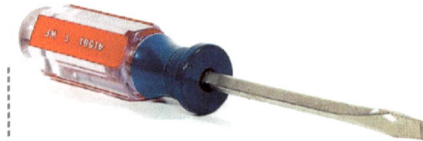

Construction Hand Tools

Screwdriver

What is a Screwdriver?

A Screwdriver is a tool, manual or powered, that it is used for turning screws. Screwdrivers have a handle and a shaft and tip that goes into the head of the screw.

When was the first Screwdriver used or invented?

Evidence shows that the first screwdrivers were used in the Middle Ages, invented in the 5th century, in Germany or France.

Sizes? Materials?

The handle is typically made of hard plastic. The shaft and tip are made of steel.

Learning Fact

Powered screwdrivers use different tips (Flat or Star) and are powered by an electric motor or batteries. Cordless drills with speed are commonly used as power

Construction Hand Tools

Construction Hand Tools

Pliers

Today We Present Series

What are Pliers?

Pliers are a hand tool used to hold objects, bend, or even compress different materials. Pliers consist of two metal sections with a plastic or covered in plastic handle and jaws.

When was the first Pliers used or invented?

Evidence shows that the first pliers were used 3,000 years before BCE (Before the common era) and in

Sizes? Materials?

Pliers are made of steel with a plastic or plastic covered handle.

Learning Fact

Modern pliers cannot be sharpened.

Architecture
For Kids 4

Today We Present Series

45

Construction Hand Tools

Construction Tools Series

Safety Goggles

What are Safety Goggles?

Safety goggles or safety glasses is a protective eyewear that surround the eye to protect it from flying debris.

When was the first Safety Goggles used or invented?

The first evidence of goggles goes back to the 1900's used by drivers or pilots, and then used in construction.

Sizes? Materials?

Safety goggles are normally made of hard plastic and in different shapes and sizes.

Learning Fact

Safety goggles are also used by rescue dogs, military, or police dogs.

Construction Hand Tools

Construction Tools Series

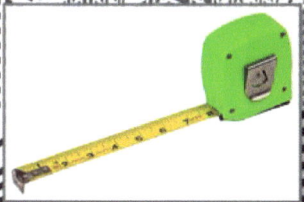

The Measuring Tape

What is the Measuring Tape?

A Measuring Tape is a soft or flexible ruler used to measure size and distance. It is used in all kinds of industries, and it is one of the most famous hand tools.

When was the first Measuring Tape used or invented?

The invention originated in Sheffield, England by James Chesterman around 1829.

Sizes? Materials?

Manufactured in different sizes and can be made of plastic, metal, fiber glass and

Learning Fact

For construction the measuring tape is made of hard plastic of metal to protect it against falls or hits.

Construction Hand Tools

Construction Hand Tools

Paintbrush

What is the Paintbrush?

A Paintbrush is a tool used to apply paint. Normally made with natural animal hair or nylon and a wood or plastic handle.

When was the first Paintbrush used or invented?

Paintbrushes were used by man as early as the Paleolithic era in around 2.5 million years ago to apply vegetables or mineral pigments.

Sizes?

Manufactured in different sizes. Thicker brushes are used for large areas and thinner are used for details.

Learning Fact

When painting large areas, paint rollers and paint sprayers are alternatives to

Construction Hand Tools

Construction Tools Series

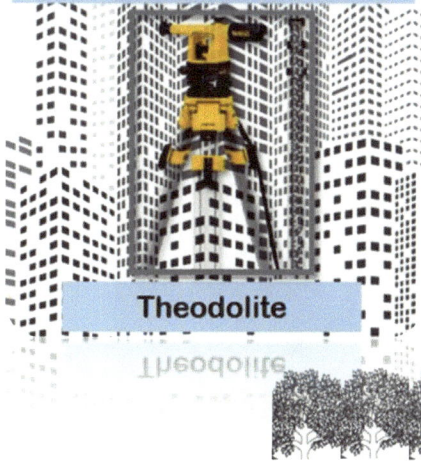

Theodolite

What is the Theodolite?

A Theodolite is an optical instrument for land surveying, but they are also used for building and roads construction.

When was the first Theodolite used or invented?

The first modern Theodolite was built in 1725 by Jonathan Sisson.

Sizes?

Manufactured in different sizes and normally made of metal and electronic components.

Learning Fact

The origin of the name is unknown.

Heavy Equipment Series

"Heavy equipment are heavy-duty vehicles. They are specially designed for completing construction tasks involving digging. Other known names for heavy equipment are heavy machines, heavy trucks, construction equipment."
Kids Encyclopedia Facts

Architecture
For Kids 4

Heavy Equipment Series

Loader

Today We Present Series

What is a Loader?

A Loader is a heavy equipment machine used in construction to move or load materials like rocks, sand, construction debris onto another piece of equipment. There are many types and sizes of loaders, and they a diesel motor.

Heavy Equipment Series

Bulldozer

What is a Bulldozer?

A Loader is a heavy equipment machine used in construction to move or load materials like rocks, sand, construction debris onto another piece of equipment. There are many types and sizes of loaders, and they a diesel motor.

Heavy Equipment Series

Heavy Equipment Series

Skid-steer loader

Heavy Equipment Series

Excavator

Today We Present Series

What is a Skid-steer Loader?

A Skid loader is a small engine powered machine with lift arms that can move material from one location to another, carry material, or load material into a truck. The first skid loader was invented by brothers Cyril and Louis Keller in 1957.

What is an Excavator?

Excavators are heavy construction equipment consisting of an arm with a bucket on a rotating platform known as the house. Excavators move with wheels or on tracks. Excavators are used in many ways, to dig holes, trenches, foundations.

Heavy Equipment Series

Heavy Equipment Series

Forklift

FORKLIFT

What is a Forklift?

A Forklift is a powered industrial truck used to lift and move materials over short distances. It was developed in the early 20th century by various companies. Forklift trucks are available in different sizes and variations and are used in different industries.

Heavy Equipment Series

Road roller

Road roller

What is a Road Roller?

A Road Roller is a compactor construction equipment used to compact (crush) gravel, concrete, or asphalt in the construction of roads. The first rollers were moved by horses that were replaced by motors in the mid-19th century.

Heavy Equipment Series

Heavy Equipment Series

Dump Truck

Heavy Equipment Series

Concrete Mixing Truck

Today We Present Series

What is a Dump Truck?

A Dump Truck known also as dumper truck or tipper truck, is used to take construction material such as gravel, sand, or waste. Because of the size and the difficulty of maintaining visual contact with people dump trucks can be a threat.

What is a Concrete Mixing Truck?

Concrete Mixing Trucks are made to mix concrete and transport it to the construction site. They can be charged with dry materials and water, with the mixing occurring during transport. In the interior of the truck a spiral blade helps to mix the concrete until it is delivered.

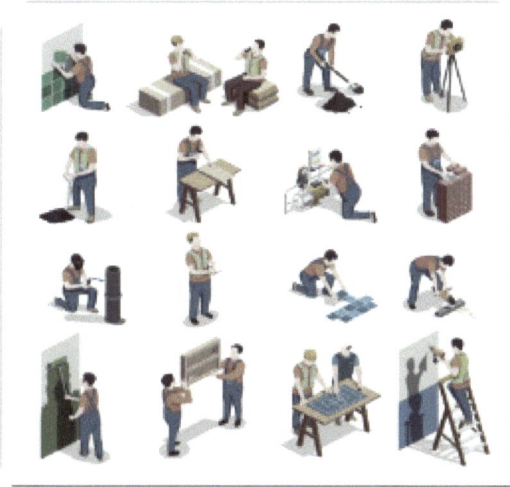

Construction Professionals

"Construction safety is very important to ensure a safe environment for the workers. All construction workers need to be educated on safety at each construction site to minimize injuries"

Kiddle.com

Construction Professionals

Construction Professionals

Bricklayer

Today We Present Series

Bricklayer

- Occupation Type: Craftsman

- Construction Worker

- Education Required: High School – Technical School.

Bricklayers build the interior and exterior walls of buildings. A bricklayer may work on new buildings, extensions, or the restoration of existing buildings. Bricklayers need to wear protective clothing, footwear, a safety helmet and sometimes safety glasses.

Principal Tools and Materials:

Do you recognize these tools and materials?

Construction Professionals

Carpenter

Today We Present Series

Carpenter

- Occupation Type: Craftsman

- Construction Worker

- Education Required: High School – Technical School.

Carpenters work in the construction industry and in the fabrication of furniture. Carpenters may use hand saws, power saws, or wood machines. Carpenters work indoors or outdoors. Since carpenters use sharp tools they need to use protective

Principal Tools and Materials:

Do you recognize these tools and materials?

Construction Professionals

Construction Professionals

Cement Mason

Today We Present Series

Cement Mason

- Occupation Type: Craftsman

- Construction Worker

- Education Required: High School – Technical School.

Cement masons pour, smooth, and finish concrete floors, sidewalks, roads, and curbs. They must be able to carry heavy materials. The work, either indoors or outdoors, may be in areas that are muddy, dusty, or dirty.

Principal Tools and Materials:

Do you recognize these tools and materials?

Construction Professionals

Construction Professionals

Drywall Installer

Today We Present Series

Drywall Installer

- Occupation Type: Craftsman

- Construction Worker

- Education Required: High School – Technical School.

A Drywall installer is someone that installs drywall to walls and ceilings inside buildings. Drywall panels are installed with screws, screws are covered with tape that is also painted. Workers spend most of the time bending, standing, or stretching.

Principal Tools and Materials:

Do you recognize these tools and materials?

Construction Professionals

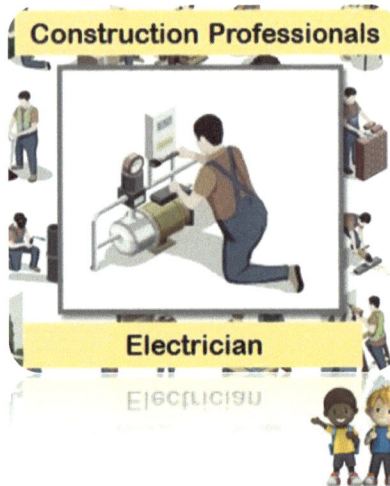

Construction Professionals

Electrician

Today We Present Series

Electrician

- Occupation Type: Craftsman

- Construction Worker

- Education Required: High School – Technical School.

Electricians design, install and maintain electric installations in houses or commercial or industrial buildings.

Principal Tools and Materials:

Do you recognize these tools and materials?

Construction Professionals

Construction Professionals

Painter

Today We Present Series

Painter

- Occupation Type: Craftsman

- Construction Worker

- Education Required: High School – Technical School.

Painters make things look clean and finished. They use paintbrushes, rollers, and power sprayers to apply paint, stain, and coatings to walls, buildings, bridges, and old kind of structures.

Principal Tools and Materials:

Do you recognize these tools and materials?

Construction Professionals

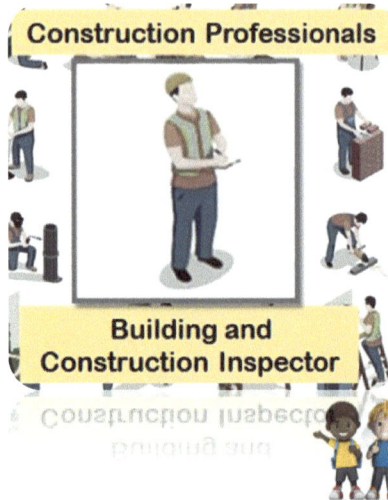

Construction Professionals

Building and Construction Inspector

Today We Present Series

Building and Construction Inspector

- Occupation Type: Craftsman

- Construction Worker

- Education Required: High School – Technical School.

A building and construction inspector normally works for a city or town and his job is to inspect buildings to be sure that they are safe to use. After the inspection is complete the building (new or used) can be sold or occupied.

Principal Tools and Materials:

Do you recognize these tools and materials?

Today We Present Series

Architecture
For Kids 4

62

Construction Professionals

Construction Professionals

Plumber

Today We Present Series

Plumber

- Occupation Type: Craftsman

- Construction Worker

- Education Required: High School – Technical School.

A plumber is a construction professional who installs and maintains pipes in our homes and businesses. Pipes need to be installed and maintained for potable water, drainage, irrigation, sewage, or other issues.

Principal Tools and Materials:

Do you recognize these tools and materials?

Construction Professionals

Construction Professionals

Surveyor

Surveyor

- Occupation Type: Craftsman

- Construction Worker

- Education Required: High School – Technical School, Associate Degree.

A surveyor is a construction professional who identifies the limits of an area of land, water, or airspace. Surveyors work with civil engineers, landscape architects, and urban planners.

Principal Tools and Materials:

Do you recognize these tools and materials?

Construction Professionals

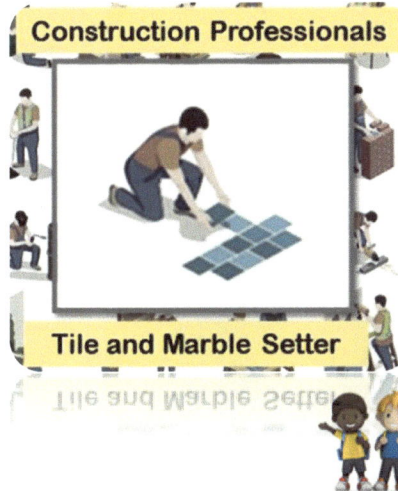

Tile and Marble Setter

Today We Present Series

Tile and Marble Setter

- Occupation Type: Craftsman

- Construction Worker

- Education Required: High School – Technical School.

A Tile and Marble setter is someone who applies hard tile (ceramic), marble, and wood tiles to walls, floors, and other surfaces. Installing tile and marble is labor intensive, workers spend much time bending, and kneeling.

Principal Tools and Materials:

Do you recognize these tools and materials?

Today We Present Series

V. Index

Photo Credits:

- **Page 7**

 Seamless urban background stock - Meranna -iStock-932306662

 Industrial Vechicles Icons, Monoline concept stock illustration - cloudnumber9 - 1159499631

 Construction workers isometric people stock illustration - Macrovector -1201248860

 Night Skyscrapers City stock illustration - imassimo82 - iStock-841828528

- **Page 9**
- Seamless urban background stock - Meranna -iStock-932306662

- **Page 10**
- Seamless urban background stock - Meranna -iStock-932306662
- Door - The copyright holder of this picture, release this work into the public domain. This applies worldwide.

- The Chair - The person who associated a work with this deed has dedicated the work to the public domain by waiving all of their rights to the work worldwide under copyright law, including all related and neighboring rights, to the extent allowed by law.

- Page 18
- Seamless urban background stock - Meranna -iStock-932306662
- The Table - The copyright holder of this picture, release this work into the public domain. This applies worldwide.

- Page 19
- Seamless urban background stock - Meranna -iStock-932306662
- The Rebar - The copyright holder of this picture, release this work into the public domain. This applies worldwide.

- Page 20
- Seamless urban background stock - Meranna -iStock-932306662
- The Elevator - The copyright holder of this picture, release this work into the public domain. This applies worldwide.

- Page 21
- Seamless urban background stock - Meranna -iStock-932306662
- The Doorbell - The copyright holder of this picture, release this work into the public domain. This applies worldwide.

- Page 22
- Seamless urban background stock - Meranna -iStock-932306662
- The Door Knocker - The copyright holder of this picture, release this work into the public domain. This applies worldwide.

- Page 23
- Seamless urban background stock - Meranna -iStock-932306662

- The Brick - The copyright holder of this picture, release this work into the public domain. This applies worldwide.

- Page 24
- Seamless urban background stock - Meranna -iStock-932306662
- Roof Tiles - The copyright holder of this picture, release this work into the public domain. This applies worldwide.

- Page 25
- Seamless urban background stock - Meranna -iStock-932306662
- The Downspout - The copyright holder of this picture, release this work into the public domain. This applies worldwide.

- Page 26
- Seamless urban background stock - Meranna -iStock-932306662
- The Rain Gutter - The copyright holder of this picture, release this work into the public domain. This applies worldwide.

- Page 27
- Seamless urban background stock - Meranna -iStock-932306662
- The Nail - The copyright holder of this picture, release this work into the public domain. This applies worldwide.

- Page 28
- Seamless urban background stock - Meranna -iStock-932306662
- The Sandpaper - The copyright holder of this picture, release this work into the public domain. This applies worldwide.

- Page 29
- Seamless urban background stock - Meranna -iStock-932306662

- The Chimney - The copyright holder of this picture, release this work into the public domain. This applies worldwide.

- Page 30
- Seamless urban background stock - Meranna -iStock-932306662
- The Storage Water Heater - The copyright holder of this picture, release this work into the public domain. This applies worldwide.

- Page 31
- Seamless urban background stock - Meranna -iStock-932306662
- The Drywall - The copyright holder of this picture, release this work into the public domain. This applies worldwide.

- Page 32
- Seamless urban background stock - Meranna -iStock-932306662
- The Wallpaper - The copyright holder of this picture, release this work into the public domain. This applies worldwide.

- Page 33
- Seamless urban background stock - Meranna -iStock-932306662
- Faux Painting - The copyright holder of this picture, release this work into the public domain. This applies worldwide.

- Page 34
- Seamless urban background stock - Meranna -iStock-932306662
- Wood - The copyright holder of this picture, release this work into the public domain. This applies worldwide.

- Page 35
- Seamless urban background stock - Meranna -iStock-932306662

- Paint - The copyright holder of this picture, release this work into the public domain. This applies worldwide.

- Page 36

Night Skyscrapers City stock illustration - imassimo82 - iStock-841828528

- Page 37
- Night Skyscrapers City stock illustration - imassimo82 - iStock-841828528
- The Trowel - The copyright holder of this picture, release this work into the public domain. This applies worldwide.

- Page 38
- Night Skyscrapers City stock illustration - imassimo82 - iStock-841828528
- The Shovel - The copyright holder of this picture, release this work into the public domain. This applies worldwide.

- Page 39
- Night Skyscrapers City stock illustration - imassimo82 - iStock-841828528
- The Pickaxe - The copyright holder of this picture, release this work into the public domain. This applies worldwide.

- Page 40
- Night Skyscrapers City stock illustration - imassimo82 - iStock-841828528
- The Wheelbarrow - The copyright holder of this picture, release this work into the public domain. This applies worldwide.

- Page 41
- Night Skyscrapers City stock illustration - imassimo82 - iStock-841828528

- The Hard Hat - The copyright holder of this picture, release this work into the public domain. This applies worldwide.

- Page 42

- Page 43

- Page 44

- Page 45

- Page 46

- Page 47

- The Measuring Tape - The copyright holder of this picture, release this work into the public domain. This applies worldwide.

- Page 48
- Night Skyscrapers City stock illustration - imassimo82 - iStock-841828528
- Paintbrush - The copyright holder of this picture, release this work into the public domain. This applies worldwide.

- Page 49
- Night Skyscrapers City stock illustration - imassimo82 - iStock-841828528
- Theodolite - The copyright holder of this picture, release this work into the public domain. This applies worldwide.

- Page 50

Industrial Vechicles Icons, Monoline concept stock illustration - cloudnumber9 - 1159499631

- Page 51
- Industrial Vechicles Icons, Monoline concept stock illustration - cloudnumber9 - 1159499631
- Loader - The copyright holder of this picture, release this work into the public domain. This applies worldwide.
- Bulldozer - The copyright holder of this picture, release this work into the public domain. This applies worldwide.

- Page 52
- Industrial Vechicles Icons, Monoline concept stock illustration - cloudnumber9 - 1159499631
- Skid Steer Loader - The copyright holder of this picture, release this work into the public domain. This applies worldwide.
- Excavator - The copyright holder of this picture, release this work into the public domain. This applies worldwide.

- Page 59
- Drywall Installer – Modified Construction workers isometric people stock illustration - Macrovector - 1201248860

- Page 60
- Electrician – Modified Construction workers isometric people stock illustration - Macrovector - 1201248860

- Page 61
- Painter – Modified Construction workers isometric people stock illustration - Macrovector - 1201248860

- Page 62
- Building and Construction Inspector – Modified Construction workers isometric people stock illustration - Macrovector -1201248860

- Page 63
- Plumber – Modified Construction workers isometric people stock illustration - Macrovector - 1201248860

- Page 64
- Surveyor – Modified Construction workers isometric people stock illustration - Macrovector - 1201248860

- Page 65
- Tile and Marble Setter – Modified Construction workers isometric people stock illustration - Macrovector -1201248860

About the Author

My story started in my childhood when I was extremely interested in Architecture. I remember using wood blocks and books to build buildings, houses, and malls. Experimenting with forms, colors, textures, and lights. Architecture is my passion, and in a way, I had the born skills to do it; like for example seeing things with more detail, or from a different perspective. Architecture is an art, as well as a discipline that helps to transform ideas into something real. This book is the result of an idea and the need to share my love and passion for this discipline.

Dr. Horacio Sanchez is an architect with over twenty years of experience in international projects. At the age of five, he was convinced that architecture was his passion and the career that he wanted to follow. Dr. Horacio likes to share his experience and expertise by mentoring and coaching colleagues and students encouraging them to show a huge passion for what they do and for what they want to accomplish. As a researcher, he is interested in the design-thinking concept and how it can be applied in the education of future generations. Thinking like a designer helps to build the skill to see things in a different way. It is not what you see, is what others do not see.